For André and Noelle

Library of Congress catalog card number: 2020941857
ISBN: 978-1-7353521-2-1 (Paperback)
978-1-7353521-5-2 (Hardback)
978-1-7353521-3-8 (Ebook)

MIKAELA WILSON
— BOOKS INC. —

NOELLE
The Best Big Sister

Written by
Mikaela Wilson

Illustrated by
Pardeep Mehra

Art Direction and Storyboards by
Mikaela Wilson

The sun is just beginning to shine
as Noelle jumps out of bed.

"Today I'm going to be a big sister!"

"Mom and Dad said we'll have a new baby today.
I'm going to be the best big sister."

Noelle brushes her teeth...

"WHOOPS!"

...and puts on her best "big sister" clothes.

She makes a pile of her favorite books
to read to the new baby.

She picks out her favorite toys to share with the new baby.

She even sets aside her favorite teddy bear to show the new baby.

Noelle hears her dad calling,

"Mom is home!"

She goes downstairs,
carrying her favorite
teddy bear.

"Noelle, come and meet the new baby,"
Mom says.

Noelle feels sad when she sees her mom holding the new baby in her arms.

She wonders if she really wants this new baby.

"That's MY mom!!!"

Noelle screams, as tears run down her face.

"Of course I'm YOUR mom, honey," her mom says,

"and I'm the new baby's mom, too."

Noelle's dad picks her up
and gives her a big hug.

That makes Noelle
feel much better.

"Would you like to hold the new baby?"
Noelle's mom asks.

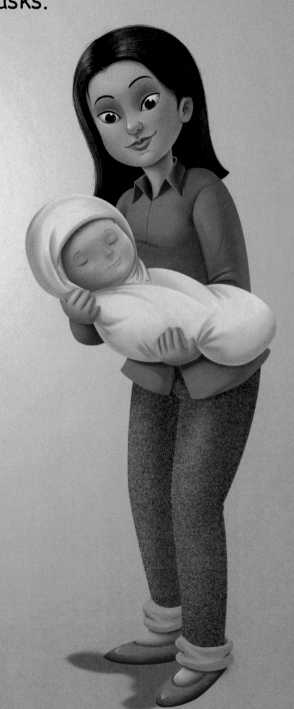

Noelle wipes away her tears.

She looks at the sweet little baby and softly says, "yes."

Noelle's dad helps her sit on the couch and hold her arms out.

Her mom gently places the baby in her arms.

Noelle's mom smiles as she helps her cradle the baby in her arms. The baby is so small and cuddly.

Noelle loves the baby.

After dinner, Noelle is ready for her usual playtime with Mom and Dad.

"Mom! Dad! Let's play!"

But her parents are busy taking care of the new baby.

Noelle sits in her room, wondering what to do.

"Wait, I can help with the new baby!"

Noelle runs into the baby's room.

"Mom, can I help feed the new baby?" she asks.
"Sure!" says Mom. She lets Noelle help hold the baby's bottle.

"Dad, can I help change the baby's diaper?" she asks. "Sure," says Dad.

Noelle gets a clean diaper and gives it to her dad.

(peeee-eww!)

Noelle even throws the dirty one in the trash.

Noelle shows the baby the books she has set aside and the toys she has picked out.

She has the best night with her mom and dad and the new baby.

Noelle even sings a sweet, bedtime song to the new baby.

Then she kisses the baby on the cheek and whispers,

"I love you, baby."

The baby coos at her and drifts off to sleep.

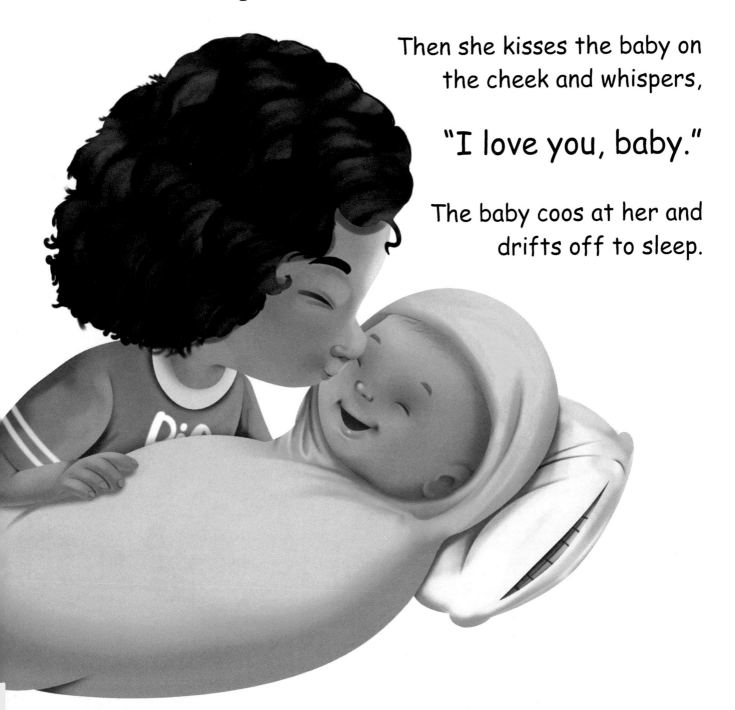